Cook Memorial Public Library

3 1122 00882 1238

P9-DFK-121

808.042 SPE   FEB 2 4 2005
Spencer, Lauren.
A step-by-step guide to
 personal writing

The Library of
Writing Skills™

A Step-by-Step
Guide to
Personal
Writing

COOK MEMORIAL LIBRARY
413 N. MILWAUKEE AVE.
LIBERTYVILLE, ILLINOIS 60048

Lauren Spencer

The Rosen Publishing Group, Inc., New York

To all of those individuals whose support and encouragement
have made the writing of personal moments so much fun

Published in 2005 by The Rosen Publishing Group, Inc.
29 East 21st Street, New York, NY 10010

Copyright © 2005 by The Rosen Publishing Group, Inc.

First Edition

All rights reserved. No part of this book may be reproduced in any form
without permission in writing from the publisher, except by a reviewer.

Library of Congress Cataloging-in-Publication Data

Spencer, Lauren.
A step-by-step guide to personal writing / Lauren Spencer.—1st ed.
    p. cm. — (The library of writing skills)
Includes bibliographical references and index.
ISBN 1-4042-0216-1 (library binding)
ISBN 1-4042- 5308-4 (pbk.)
6-pack ISBN 1-4042-5314-9
1. English language—Rhetoric. 2. Autobiography—Authorship. 3. Report
writing. I. Title. II. Series: Spencer, Lauren, Library of writing skills.
PE1408.S6646 2005
808'.042—dc22

                                                          2004002686

Manufactured in the United States of America

Table of Contents

Introduction

Personal writing is a great way for an author to communicate how he or she feels about the world. Authors can find many ways to express themselves by writing their personal thoughts, either for their own private journals or to share with others. Whether kept private or not, every personal writing style offers a distinct view into the mind of its author. Personal writing gives both the reader (if there is one) and the author a chance to understand more fully the thoughts of its creator.

Personal writing styles can vary. They can take the form of a narrative tale, which uses traditional storytelling techniques like setting, characterization, and dialogue; or poetry and free verse, which are more freestyle forms of expression. Letters are also a fun form in which to write about and share a personal moment, while journal writing is a personal expression of the author's innermost thoughts, often recorded with privacy in mind.

Whatever form of personal writing you choose, your aim is to find pleasure in your expression. Personal writing depends on observations and thoughts. It does not rely heavily on facts or research. Personal writing can be a very enjoyable way to express yourself because your aim is to write from the heart. It can serve all kinds of functions, from remembering and recording memories, to communicating feelings and emotions, to sharing an event with a friend.

This book will examine the various ways that personal writing can take shape—from choosing a topic and style, writing it out, and then polishing and presenting your work. Ultimately, your goal is to encourage the writer inside of you while enjoying the journey of creative expression.

1

Prewriting

Whether you're writing on your own or you've been assigned a personal writing project, a basic, straightforward narrative is an excellent way to express your thoughts. A narrative details an event or a series of events in the order in which it happened. The best way to write an effective narrative is to choose a subject you feel strongly about. Although many topics would make great writing subjects, decide on one idea to explore.

Since personal writing depends on your connection to your subject, choose a topic that allows you to fully express yourself. It's fun to think about a variety of ideas for writing assignments, since topics often revolve around things you have enjoyed, such as an event in your own life. Although this type of writing requires little research beyond examining items that may jog your memory, begin with some facts to help you create an interesting piece.

Focus on moments in which every one of your senses was alive.

KEY

✔ **Survey the variety of ideas and topics that are available to you.**

✔ **Choose a topic.**

✔ **Find and create details to support your chosen topic.**

This can range from a memory of a birthday party or celebration, to your first meeting with someone, to an especially scary experience such as spending a night alone in a strange place. Pull out a blank piece of paper and begin the brainstorming process of prewriting, or freely jotting down your ideas.

One way to get your thoughts moving is to organize them in a sensory chart, based around the experience that you intend to recall in your story. Along the top of the first line of the page, write out the five senses (sight, smell, hearing, touch, taste), then list situations where you've felt each of those senses in an extreme way. Include as many details as you can. You will probably come across at least one event on your list that really satisfies all of the senses and would therefore make an exciting topic for your piece.

Gathering Details

Once you've decided on your topic, you can focus on the other elements surrounding the experience. At this stage, you should gather all the material for your writing. Think about people who can answer questions about the moment you are exploring, such as someone else who was there or a person whom you told about the event. Examining photo albums might also be helpful.

You can also find interesting information for your writing by searching the world around you. This may spark additional ideas. Books, music, and movies can remind you of details about your topic, so if something pops into your head while you are reading, listening, or watching, write it down. Think about what music might have been playing during your experience, or how the event may remind you of a movie or a book's storyline.

You can also ask yourself questions about the topic. Use a tape recorder or a pad of paper and pen and try "interviewing" yourself about the subject as if you were a stranger wanting to know more about the experience. Imagine that someone is making a movie of your story. How would you describe the situation to him or her? How would the setting appear? Write down all the details.

These warm-up techniques will bring your topic into focus and give you a strong foundation on which to build your writing. Make sure the subject you've chosen is streamlined into one thought. This means that your topic should contain just one moment in time rather than bounce from topic to topic. Focusing on one event is important. It helps avoid confusion so that you don't get offtrack while writing.

Thinking Differently

ASK YOURSELF

❑ Have I chosen a topic that excites me?

❑ Is my subject focused on only one event?

❑ Is my topic rich with detail?

❑ Does my topic excite the senses?

Considering a topic from a different viewpoint might help you notice details you've taken for granted because you're so close to the subject. As a creative writing exercise, try taking your topic and writing about it from the viewpoint of someone (or something!) else.

For instance, how would your dog or cat see the situation, or your mom, or a celebrity? If you are writing about your birthday, consider writing about it from the point of view of another person at the party, such as your best friend, a late or unexpected guest, or an outsider looking in. You might even try writing from the viewpoint or perspective of an inanimate object, such as a piñata or a Christmas tree! Play around with different variations and see if any spark your interest. You'll be surprised to learn how changing the point of view in any situation can drastically alter the story's focus, drama, or creative expression.

The Subjective Voice

In a personal writing piece, authors often use a subjective voice. This means that the piece is written in the first person (I) and reflects the opinions and attitudes of the writer toward the event. The subjective voice gives the writer an opportunity to pour his or her heart and soul into the piece without holding back. Whether this creation will be read by anyone else or not, the point of the subjective voice is to express the author's thoughts with freedom and honesty.

2

Different Writing Styles

All personal writing comes from an author's own life and connects to his or her own experiences. Teachers often tell students to write like they speak. In the case of personal writing, this is especially true. Various styles can be used when writing from a personal perspective.

Each of the following styles serves a specific purpose that makes it individual to the writer. Personal narratives tell a story. Personal letters share an event with someone else. Poetry expresses experiences that may be shared with others or kept private. Journal writing reflects the writer's innermost thoughts and is often written only for the author. Before starting your personal draft, pinpoint which style you'll be using for your piece. If the first one doesn't suit your story, try another.

KEY

✔ **Personal writing styles often lend themselves to any story.**

✔ **Trying various styles can help you find your author's voice.**

Narratives

The narrative is probably the most traditional personal writing style. It has a specific format that includes a beginning, a middle, and an end. The personal narrative is written in the first person (I) and is the retelling of an event using story elements such as setting, character, and plot, or the series of actions that make up your story. Sometimes the word "memoir" is used with this type of writing. A memoir is an autobiographical piece that spans different moments in the author's life. A personal narrative is different from a memoir because it highlights only one specific moment.

A great way to get your topic organized is to use a five Ws chart to outline your draft. By using this method, you can fill in the details of your experience.

Five Ws Chart

Topic: "Visiting My Uncle"

Questions	Answers
Who?	Me, Sean Hughes
What?	I was flying on an airplane
When?	Over the holidays
Where?	Going to Puerto Rico
Why?	To visit my uncle

ASK YOURSELF

❑ Have I chosen a style that best reflects my personal experience?

❑ Could my piece be written in all the various ways mentioned in this chapter?

Letters

Writing a letter to a friend is a fun, expressive way to share an experience. Keep a friendly tone and include a joke, a story, a poem, or a sketch. Remember that there are five formatting requirements that should be followed when writing a letter. The heading at the top right-hand corner needs to include your address and the date. A salutation at the beginning is where you greet the person to whom you're writing, using "Dear so-and-so." Write the salutation at the left-hand margin below the heading, and use a comma after the name. The body of the letter includes your thoughts and ideas. Use short paragraphs to hold the reader's attention, and skip one line between paragraphs for easier reading. The letter's closing includes your sign-off and signature and is usually written about two lines below the body.

When writing a letter, you can imagine that your reader is listening to your story. Be as detailed as you can about your topic. Using exclamation marks and other punctuation can help to get your point across. You can also use rhetorical questions, which are questions asked for effect with no expected answers. Personal questions aimed at the person receiving the letter are also a thoughtful way to connect to your reader. If you are sending your letter through electronic mail, you need to add a title in the subject line.

333 Everywhere St.

Almostville, USA 33345

January 6, 2005

Dear Layne,

I just returned from Puerto Rico, where I was visiting my uncle for the holidays. It was difficult getting there because the airplane ride was a nightmare! It made me remember the first time I was on a plane when I was ten years old. This time it wasn't so much that I didn't know what to expect as it was the huge storm that was approaching.

Right after we took off, the plane started bouncing. At one point, I made a loud noise, and a passenger stared at me with an angry look. I felt sort of silly, but what was her problem? I mean, hadn't she ever seen anyone startled before? Actually, I think she was just as afraid as I was.

Although it seemed like forever, we finally did touch down in Puerto Rico. How was your holiday? Write me back and let me know!

Sincerely,

Sean

Poetry

Poetry is a unique form of personal writing. A poem looks different from prose because it is written in stanzas, or divisions named for the number of lines they contain, whereas prose pieces are written in paragraphs. Poetry depends on rich descriptions to bring a situation to life. A poem comes primarily from the author's innermost feelings. Many different styles of poetry exist. For a full range of choices, look at Web sites such as the Academy of American Poets at www.poets.org or in books about poetry.

poetry Some Types of Traditional Poetry

Ballad: A ballad is a poem that tells a story, such as "All the World's a Stage" by sixteenth-century English poet William Shakespeare.

Blank Verse: Blank verse is unrhymed poetry with meter.

Elegy: An elegy is a sad poem, such as "A Refusal to Mourn the Death, by Fire, of a Child in London" by the twentieth-century English poet Dylan Thomas.

Epic: An epic is a long story poem that usually tells about the adventures of a hero, such as *The Odyssey* by the ancient Greek poet Homer.

Free Verse: Free verse is poetry that does not follow a specific meter or rhyme scheme. See an example of free verse on page 15.

Haiku: A haiku is a form of Japanese poetry that is three lines in length, each line with a specific number of syllables. See an example of a haiku on page 16.

Lyric: A lyric is a short poem that expresses personal feelings and emotions.

Ode: An ode is a long poem that is rich in poetic devices and imagery, such as "Ode to the West Wind" by eighteenth-century English poet Percy Bysshe Shelley.

Sonnet: A sonnet is a fourteen-line poem, such as "What Lips My Lips Have Kissed, and Where, and Why" by nineteenth-century American poet Edna St. Vincent Millay.

Traditional poems have a regular beat with a set length to each line and are usually rhymed. Most contemporary poetry is written in free verse, meaning that there is no regular rhythm and rhyme.

A free-verse poem is one in which the poet gathers related thoughts, allowing the lines to end where they feel natural and effective. Free-verse poetry does not require any set meter (a measured rhythm) or rhyme scheme. Example:

Acrostic Poems

An acrostic poem is one that uses the letters of a word (in this case "airplane") to begin each line.

A jolt like thunder
I s all I feel
R ight as I'm settling into my seat.
P ulling a sound
L ouder than I'd expected
A ll the way from the inside of me, and I
N otice that a woman in front is
  giving me a look that
E xpresses exactly how freaked
  out I am.

Sky so blue
floating above the clouds.
White, rough,
the plane bumps.
Suddenly,
a pair of eyes behind glasses
look at me hard and hold me in their sight.
I realize that I must have let out a scream
as the bump
bounced me into the land of scared.

A haiku is a type of Japanese poem that is three lines in length. The first line contains five syllables; the second, seven; and the third, five. Although the haiku form was once reserved for expressing themes about nature, this format is now used to express almost anything. Example:

> What a rush I feel,
> When the airplane soars madly.
> Over clouds it dips.

Onomatopoeia is not a type of poetry, but a literary device often used by poets that uses words that sound like the noise an object would make. Although it is often used when writing poetry, onomatopoeia can also be used in prose writing. Example:

> Roaring, the engines lift the giant into the sky.
> Bing-bong, the seatbelt signs go off.
> Click, click, click, the food cart rolls
> down the aisle.
> And "waaaaa," a baby screams.

Journal Writing

Journal writing is a form of personal composition that is often kept private, though it can be a great resource for any writer. Keeping a journal can help a writer maintain his or her focus so that a situation can be better understood. Attempt different writing styles in your journal, such as poetry or short stories. Writing in a journal is good practice for putting pen to paper on a daily basis and can help you become a better writer.

The Sound of Poetry

Poetry often sounds best when it's read aloud. Here are a few techniques to make your poetry sing.

- Repetition of the same words at the beginning of each line, such as "I can…I can…I can," gives the poem rhythm.

- When you use words that start with the same consonant, it is called alliteration. "The *plane performed circles in the *sky, *shining *superbly with *ferocious *force."

- When you use words that have the same vowel sounds, it is called assonance, which also brings a rhyming feel to the poem. "When the airplane *flew* into the *blue*, I knew that we'd all go, '*Whew*.'"

Establish a regular time to write in your journal each day or evening, and it will become a habit. Make sure the time and place where you choose to write is convenient and quiet. While some people write while it's noisy, others need complete silence in order to concentrate.

When keeping a journal, begin by writing for a set amount of time each day. Five to ten minutes is a good start. After a few weeks, increase your writing time to fifteen to twenty minutes. After a while, your writing will improve, as will your fluency as a writer. Remember to date each entry. Example:

December 18, 2005

Today we flew to Puerto Rico to see Uncle Sal.

The flight was scary. It made me feel that I can get

through anything as long as I remain calm. I think mom was as freaked out as I was about the bumpy flight. Although she was pretending to be asleep, I saw her foot wiggling rapidly like she was nervous. At one point, I felt angry because a woman started staring at me.

Anyway, when we landed, Uncle Sal was waiting. Puerto Rico is beautiful, and the ocean is right outside of his house. I'll have to investigate the surroundings tomorrow; now I'm exhausted.

A "dialogue" journal is one that is passed between friends or family to share ideas. Example:

January 10

Kendra,

Yesterday, when I was reading the Harry Potter book, I thought about how weird it would be to live away from my family, like Harry does at Hogwarts. When I visited my Uncle Sal in Puerto Rico, I tried to convince one of my cousins to come live with us in Johnson Springs. Although you could tell he thought that it was a great idea, he didn't want to leave his home. I had never really thought about it from his viewpoint until I was reading the Harry Potter book.

Although those guys seem to have fun in the book, I don't think I'd want to go to a boarding school. What do you think?

Sincerely,

Sean

January 13

Sean,

I know what you mean about boarding school! My mom told me that she lived at her school when she was in college, but she said that by the time you're that old, it's a cool thing to do. I definitely wouldn't want to leave home right now, though. Speaking of Harry Potter, I love that part where they are in the forest with those magical horses. Have you ever gone horseback riding?

Sincerely,

Kendra

There are as many methods for writing expressive pieces as there are ideas. Be sure to try different techniques depending on your topic and your audience. If the first one fails to interest you, try another.

Allow yourself to explore your author's voice. This is the inner voice inside of you that is yours alone. Your author's voice is what will allow you to express yourself as a creative individual.

3

Writing Your First Draft

In personal writing, the story's viewpoint is subjective, meaning that it is written from the author's perspective and in the first person. This is what establishes its mood, or tone. Personal writing can have a tone that is humorous or serious, depending on how it is presented. As you write your draft, pretend that you are telling your story to a friend. This technique will help your writer's voice and tone shine through more easily. Overall, a personal story is about the richness of its descriptions. This is why the five senses and the five *W*s work so well to help personal writing reach a height of expression.

No matter what style you use, include plenty of details. There are several methods to gather and specify your thoughts before you write your draft. One method is to create a list or a cluster chart where you write exact details about the event (see example, page 21).

KEY

✔ **Focus your author's voice.**

✔ **Establish your view-point and tone.**

✔ **Begin writing.**

CLUSTER CHART

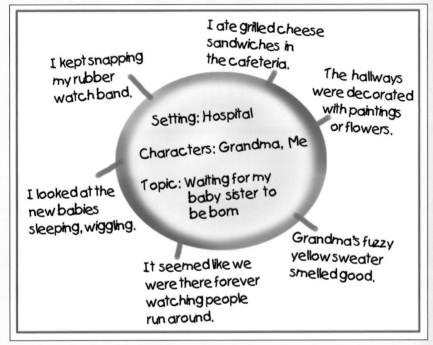

I ate grilled cheese sandwiches in the cafeteria.

I kept snapping my rubber watch band.

The hallways were decorated with paintings or flowers.

Setting: Hospital

Characters: Grandma, Me

Topic: Waiting for my baby sister to be born

I looked at the new babies sleeping, wiggling.

Grandma's fuzzy yellow sweater smelled good.

It seemed like we were there forever watching people run around.

Where to Begin

As you write your draft, think about how you'd like to introduce your subject. No matter what writing style you use, you'll need to pick an interesting point from which to begin your story. Sometimes an author will begin in the middle of the action and then offer details about how he or she ended up there. Another might begin his or her story at its end and explain the events in reverse. In other cases, authors tell their stories in chronological order describing the situation from the beginning to the end. Think about your topic and then decide which format is most suitable for engaging the reader.

Rearranging Things

Good writers sometimes rearrange the order of facts or other information in a story or poem to capture a reader's interest. Try the following methods.

Order of importance: Instead of arranging information chronologically, try arranging the details of your narrative in the order of greatest importance.

Compare and contrast: Explain the details of an event by comparing it to another one that is similar or to one that is very different.

Start at the climax: Start your story by beginning with the most important details, or reverse this method and recall some subtle details first, working your way to an exciting finish.

Example: Starting in the middle for a narrative

> They were behind the glass window, wiggling and crying. I'd never seen so many babies in one place! I was standing there because I'd gotten up to take a walk down the hallway of the hospital after my grandmother had asked me to stop making so much noise. I'd been nervously snapping a rubber watchband against my wrist for the last hour. I really didn't notice that I'd been doing it, but we were both impatiently waiting for my baby sister to be born. It seemed like we'd been waiting forever!
>
> We arrived at the hospital around two o'clock that morning and now it was five AM. We knew that everything was fine because a nurse had come and told us so, but

we were still worried. It was strangely quiet in hallways, which were decorated with paintings of huge flowers in bright colors like incredibly blue blues and extra-orange oranges. I was glad that my grandmother had worn her fuzzy sweater because it felt so nice when I put my head down on her shoulder. The only time we'd moved out of our seats was when we'd gone to the cafeteria to eat breakfast. Since they didn't have the kind of cereal I liked, I ordered a grilled cheese sandwich.

Finally, after I'd looked at the infants for a while, I returned to find my grandmother speaking with a nurse. My baby sister had just been born!

Example: Starting at the end for a personal letter

2304 Happy Lane

Supersville, Everywhere

01920

January 10, 2005

Dear Sarah,

We just returned home with my baby sister and she's a beauty! Her eyes are green and her hair is curly. Her name is Phoebe and everyone loves her, though she doesn't do much of anything yet. While I watch her sleep, it reminds me of all the other little babies I saw at the hospital the morning she was born.

My grandmother and I were there for what seemed like forever waiting for my mom to give birth. I had been annoying my grandmother by snapping a rubber watch band against my wrist (I didn't mean to!) after we had returned from the cafeteria where we ate breakfast. I had decided to take a walk around the hallways, which were decorated with colorful paintings of flowers, when I ended up staring through the glass at all the sleepy newborns. It seemed so strange.

Finally, after I had returned from my walk, a nurse told us that Phoebe had been born. Do you remember when your little brother was born? Write me back.

Sincerely,
Audrey

Example: A chronological poem

The doors open wide
at two o'clock in the morning
as mom rolls into the hospital
ready to deliver my baby sister.

Grandma, daddy, and I trail along behind.
Big, loud, blue, orange, red flowers
jump off the wall
as my mom and dad disappear into a room
just for new moms.
I put my head on grandma's fuzzy sweater
and dream of tiny babies.

Many hours later,
there she is:
the one and only Phoebe.

Time to Write

Once you have decided how you'd like to begin your draft and have your notes handy, you're ready to write. Find a place to concentrate to ensure that you'll have enough time to finish your draft. Don't concern yourself with spelling or punctuation at this point. Let your ideas and writing flow freely. With personal writing in particular, it is important to keep going until all of your ideas are incorporated into your draft. You will have a chance to make corrections and add details later.

Follow your train of thought until you've come to its end. Your writing may seem to have a life of its own. You'll remember details and moments that you may have forgotten about earlier. Write everything down, because once you've started, you'll probably find that you don't want to stop until everything's been told. Follow the story to its natural conclusion, like any journey. Fasten your seatbelt and let go!

ASK YOURSELF

- ☐ Am I being true to my memories and personal viewpoint?
- ☐ Is my writing focused on one specific subject?
- ☐ Is there a natural flow to my writing?
- ☐ Have I included everything I remembered that was related to my subject?

Figures of Speech

With all good writing, it's important to use effective figurative language to describe an event. Listed below are some useful figures of speech that will enhance any writing. Figurative language uses descriptive devices that should be added sparingly. If a writer overuses figurative language in his or her work, he or she will only weaken its appeal and drama.

Hyperbole: An exaggerated statement that "stretches" the truth.
The paintings on the wall were so bright that you needed sunglasses just to look at them.

Personification: Giving human characteristics to something that is not human.
The grilled cheese sandwich in the cafeteria cried out to be eaten.

Simile: To compare two different things using "like" or "as."
My grandmother's fuzzy sweater was as soft as a pillow.

Metaphor: To compare two different things without using "like" or "as."
My grandmother's fuzzy sweater was a soft pillow.

Looking Through the Lens

When someone makes a movie, that person is able to look through the camera lens and choose whether to zoom into the action or bring the angle out to view a larger scene. Often in a movie, you'll get both viewpoints: the close-up and the wide-angle. You can also use this technique in writing.

Think of something you do every day, such as brushing your teeth, and write about it using both of these viewpoints. First, describe the moment from very close (maybe with a description of the toothbrush) and then zoom out to reveal a wider angle. To do this, you might describe who is holding the toothbrush and what he or she looks like or how the room appears. Next, reverse your viewpoint again and zoom in for another close-up. Again, using words as your "camera," describe what you see.

Most of all, your personal writing should sound like you. Be yourself. If you aren't happy with your piece, rework it. Cross out sentences that don't work and rewrite them. Examine your piece to make sure it follows a logical order and has plenty of descriptive details. You can also use figurative language to help enhance your writer's voice. We will work closely on these points in the next chapter.

4 Revising Your First Draft

Since personal writing is primarily focused on individual experiences, it is not necessary to support it with facts. But you do need to give your readers enough detail that they feel connected to your story or poem. Even poetry requires a specific point of view that can be followed easily. If you are writing a journal entry, you'll still want to write clear descriptions.

As you begin revising your draft, keep in mind that you will have time to make spelling, grammar, and punctuation corrections later. At this stage of the process, search for places to make your story clearer, bolder, or livelier. Revising means revisiting your work and looking at it with a fresh eye. Pretend that you've never seen the writing before and find places to add interesting details.

You also want to make sure that the flow of your writing proceeds smoothly. With any type of writing, a good way to check its flow is by reading it aloud to your-

KEY

✔ **Bring your personal piece into sharp focus.**

✔ **Polish details to bring your writing to life.**

✔ **Examine and improve your sentence structure.**

self or to others. If you are sharing your work with someone, make sure he or she understands that what you are reading is a draft. Personal writing is very creative, so ensure that anyone who reads your work at this stage respects what you are doing.

As you read your writing, make notes about sections where more description and detail might improve it.

Climb Inside

Find a specific moment in the story where you can "climb inside" of it to expand its detail. Example:

> When I was eight, I was determined to see if Santa Claus was an actual person. On Christmas Eve, I pretended I was asleep in my bed, and then, when I thought everyone else was too, I went downstairs and sat down next to the Christmas tree. I thought that since I was partly hidden by the tree, if Santa did come through the door (because we didn't have a chimney), he wouldn't see me.
>
> The lights on the tree were twinkling brightly. I started staring at them. Suddenly I felt like I was in a trance. I noticed that the star, which was made

of gold foil, had a little angel on it. I thought I
saw her wink at me. I continued looking and
noticed that her hair was golden, just like the
star, and that her tiny wings were made of gauze.
Just when I thought she was about to speak, I
heard a loud noise.

Stretching the Moment

One way to add extra suspense to a story is to draw out an edgy or tense
moment. Find a place in your story where an important event is taking
place and then make it twice as long as it would normally be. Think about
when you drop something made of glass and it seems as if it takes forever
to hit the ground. Apply that same theory to your story. Example:

The noise was coming from outside. It could
have been Santa coming through the door or it could
have been a burglar. I was paralyzed, not knowing
what to do. Footsteps came closer. I felt a little
sweat run down my back as the sound of shoes moved
right outside the door. My heart was pounding so
loudly that I was sure whoever was out there could
hear me. What if it was Santa?
  Suddenly I didn't really want to know if Santa
was real or not. The doorknob rattled, first slowly,
then quickly, and then it stopped. I couldn't tell if

the door was opening or not because it was so dark.
I thought I was going to faint.

Inner and Outer Dialogue

What we say both inside our heads—whether memories or reactions to the moment—or out loud to others can also add more detail to a story. Example:

As the door started to open, I remembered the time I asked my mom why it was all right for a strange man, even if it was Santa Claus, to come into our house while we were sleeping. She was quiet for a minute and then told me that Santa was only there to give, not to take away. But as I sat on the floor, I was sure that it was not a good thing for someone to come through that door. I suddenly felt as if my Christmas was ruined. How was I going to get out of this? I thought of all sorts of excuses, like I'd only come down for a glass of water or that I wanted to check to make sure all the lights were turned off.

Suddenly, in a flash, the door opened. I cried out, "Who are you? Go away!" But then I saw that it was my dad.

He froze like a statue and said, "Reece, what are you doing?" I didn't know what to say, except to ask

him the same question. He told me that he'd gone
outside to make sure that Santa would have a smooth
landing on our lawn since it was covered with
decorations. I don't know if I believed him, but
I was relieved that it was him who'd come through
the door.

Sentence Structure

To make your writing more interesting, it's important to use a variety sentence structures. Except in the case of poetry, where you typically write in lines as opposed to complete sentences, your prose can be varied using both complex and compound sentences.

Complex Sentence

When you take a thought, or clause, that cannot stand alone—a dependent clause—and add it into a complete sentence, the sentence is called a complex sentence. Example:

ASK YOURSELF

☐ Is there a natural flow to my writing?

☐ Are there enough details to bring it to life?

☐ Does my piece reflect my individual experience?

Our house, which does not have a fireplace, better have a big enough door for Santa to fit through.

While the sentence "Our house better have a big enough door for Santa to fit through" is complete on its own, adding the dependent clause "which does not have a fireplace" adds a detail that gives the reader valuable information.

Compound Sentence

Joining two complete sentences that have both a subject and a verb creates a compound sentence. Either by using a semicolon or a conjunction ("and," "or," "but," or in this case, "so"), you can create a compound sentence. Example:

There are big Christmas ornaments decorating our front lawn; it would be hard for Santa to park his sleigh there.

Or use a conjunction:

There are big Christmas ornaments decorating our front lawn, so it would be hard for Santa to park his sleigh there.

Varying your sentence structure (as well as the length of individual sentences) will help give your writing more rhythm. Be sure to examine the individual sentences that make up your story, poem, or journal entry for places where improvements can be made.

5 Proofreading and Editing

If you've written a personal narrative or a poem, think about a title that would best work to reflect its content. Your title should contain enough information that potential readers will be curious about the piece and want to read it. Titles are not necessary for letters or journal entries.

For all types of writing, it is crucial to check spelling. If you've written your piece on the computer, then use the spell-check function. If your work is handwritten, then examine the piece and circle any questionable words. Then, look those words up in the dictionary. If you find that you've used the same words repeatedly, circle them and then use a thesaurus to find alternative words. A thesaurus is a book of words and a list of synonyms that can be used instead. Synonyms are different words that have the same meaning as the one you were planning to use. For example, some synonyms

KEY

✔ **Give your draft a title.**

✔ **Complete a spelling and grammar check.**

✔ **Have someone read and check your draft.**

for the verb "laugh" are "giggle," "snicker," "cackle," and "guffaw."

Correct punctuation is also something you'll want to review. Although free-verse poetry does not require you to capitalize the first letter of each line, you do need to ensure that punctuation is used at the end of a complete thought. Personal writing can often contain emotional moments, and therefore you might want to use exclamation points to deliver your message.

Double Check

Because personal writing is something that comes from your heart and has to do with individual experiences, it's important to do a final edit with another person. In the case of a letter, read it aloud to a friend or family member before recopying it or typing it. Also, make sure you have dated it and included the correct address.

If you are writing a journal, you may not want to share your work with anyone. However, it's always a good idea to find a willing audience to share a narrative or poem before writing its final version.

You can pair up with a partner to exchange pieces or take turns reading your work aloud to a group. Even with poetry, the writing needs to make sense, so be certain to ask whether your point has come across the way you wanted it to. Explain to your partner that you want him or her to share such thoughts in a constructive way.

ASK YOURSELF

- ☐ Have I made all the spelling and grammar changes on my page?

- ☐ Have I used a variety of descriptive words?

- ☐ Do I convey the excitement and importance of my personal moment in the writing?

Constructive criticism should be useful and thoughtful.

A good way to explain constructive criticism is to hand out a list of items for the audience to review. They can make notes on each point to exchange with you once the reading is over.

Constructive Criticism

- What part of the writing do you remember most and why?
- How can the writer improve any specific section of his/her work?

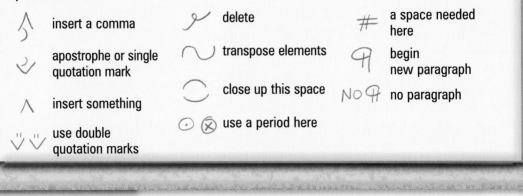

Proofreading Symbols

If you've given your piece to someone and he or she has corrected it with proofreading marks, here is a guide to let you know what those symbols mean.

insert a comma	delete	a space needed here
apostrophe or single quotation mark	transpose elements	begin new paragraph
insert something	close up this space	no paragraph
use double quotation marks	use a period here	

- What part of the writing leaves you wanting more?
- How can the writer add details to bring his or her piece to life?
- Does the title capture the point of the piece?

Being a Good Listener

It's important to know how to listen when someone is presenting his or her writing. Here are a few tips to keep in mind:

- Look directly at the speaker.
- Notice how the speaker uses his or her voice and hands.
- Write down any words that are new to you or that are confusing.
- Ask the reader questions about anything that is unclear.

Proofreading your work usually involves reading it several times. Be sure to read your writing out loud at least once so that you could hear places where it might sound awkward. Read your work line by line, and examine each sentence carefully. Make notes in the margins of words or sentences that you want to delete or replace. Note the structure and length of each sentence, and check for missing words. Finally, examine your work for errors in spelling, punctuation, or capitalization.

Presentation

Now that your personal piece has been completely written, it's time to put it into its final form by rewriting it. No matter what style you're writing in, make sure your name is somewhere on the page. It's important that you, the author, get credit for your work.

If your piece is a personal narrative, transfer your writing onto clean white paper using blue or black ink. If you're typing it into a computer, use a clear, easy-to-read font style. If a picture could add detail to your story, include one in a way that will not distract the reader.

If you are rewriting a poem, you can make its presentation fancier by using colored paper. You can also use more freedom in font style, size, and ink color when presenting poetry. If you are trying to convey a specific message with your poem, think about an appropriate way to present it. For instance, if you've written about a star, use a stencil to trace a star and write the poem inside it. For letter writing, paper and font

KEY

✔ **Add final touches to your piece, such as a title.**

✔ **Think about forums where you would like to share your work.**

style are also important. Maybe the person you're sending the letter to has a favorite color that can be used for paper or ink. You can also look into finding pictures to add to the story. If you are describing a vacation, you could include a souvenir inside the letter, such as a leaf, a photograph, or a postcard.

In the case of journal writing, it's always nice to have a special book to record your thoughts. Find a blank book that appeals to you at a stationery shop, or go to an art supply store and buy one with a plain cover that you can personalize yourself.

Places to Share

Personal writing can be shared in a variety of ways. These range from putting together anthologies, which are collections of writings, to readings for friends and family. If you want to send your work into the world beyond your immediate acquaintances, you can ask an adult to help you search the Internet for magazines or newspapers that publish like-minded, age-appropriate works. Also, check out other options in the Getting Published section at the rear of this book. If you decide to send your work to any of these places, follow their submission rules closely. Following submission guidelines carefully (even when submitting student writing!) can help any writer make it past the rejection pile.

A more immediate way to gather feedback is to hold a reading with other writers and invite people to listen to your

Story Chain

Creating a story chain can be a fun way to write by collaborating with others. This means that you have many writers working on one piece. One way to get this idea in motion is to think about a memory and write a narrative paragraph about it. Send that paragraph, either through the mail with a self-addressed stamped envelope (SASE) or via e-mail with your return address included, to a friend. Ask your friend to add his or her own memory having to do with the same subject and then send it on to one of his or her friends to continue the chain. Do this until you have at least ten contributors.

Decide on the number of participants you want to include at the beginning and include a checklist for writers to mark off when they're done, so the writing doesn't just float around forever. When the last person has checked off number ten on the tally sheet, have him or her put the writing into the SASE and pop it into the mail or have the person e-mail the document back to you. When you receive it, you can make copies for all the writers or send each a copy via e-mail. What you receive will contain ten different perspectives on one cool topic!

work. To get inspiration, you can attend author readings at local bookstores. Check the newspaper or call the store directly to see if any in your area hold such events. Going to public readings is a great way to see how authors present their works.

Places to Look

The magazine *Stone Soup* publishes writing by young people. It also has a Web site that offers students different opportunities to submit their writing. You can find it at www.stonesoup.com. The Web site also has links to other locations featuring publishing opportunities. Scholastic Inc. also has a Web site (www.scholastic.com) where you and your teacher can share your work and get feedback from professional and student writers.

We have discussed many different types of personal writing in this book, and hopefully, there are plenty of ideas that sound appealing. Personal writing can be more than just a way of expressing yourself. It can be a way to communicate with distant family and friends, a way of rethinking your thoughts and ideas, or a therapeutic method of sorting out your day. Whatever your reason for beginning your creative journey, speak your mind and express yourself!

ASK YOURSELF

☐ Is my piece ready to be presented?

☐ What did I learn about myself while writing my piece?

☐ What other styles of personal writing would I like to try?

Glossary

anthology A collection of poems, essays, lyrics, and stories.

author's voice The distinct style and personality that every writer brings to his or her work.

characters The people who populate a story.

chronological Relating to the order in which events occurred.

cluster chart Graphic organizer used to gather thoughts and details for writing.

complex sentence A sentence formed by one independent clause and one or more dependent clauses.

compound sentence A sentence in which two independent clauses are joined by a coordinate conjunction.

conjunction A word used to connect individual words or groups of words.

dependent clause A clause that cannot stand on its own as a complete sentence.

dialogue Conversation between characters in a piece of work.

figure of speech A device used by authors to create a special meaning for their readers, such as personification, metaphor, and simile.

first draft The first version of a story, written without concern about mistakes.

font Style of type used in printing.

format Style or manner of a piece of writing.

grammar The guidelines and rules writers follow in order to speak and write in an acceptable manner.

hyperbole Extreme exaggeration or overstatement used for emphasis.

inner dialogue A character's thoughts presented in a way that reveals the person is talking to him or herself.

journal A daily record of happenings.

memoir A record of events based on the writer's personal observations, experiences, or knowledge.

narrative An account of an event.

paragraph A passage of writing of one or more sentences that contains a series of related thoughts.

personification A figure of speech in which a nonhuman object is given human characteristics.

phrase A group of related words that do not express complete thoughts.

plot The plan of action in a story.

poetry A piece of writing written in stanzas or verses.

point of view The focus of the story from a character's perspective.

proofreading Reviewing the final version for errors.

revise To go back and make changes as needed.

rhetorical question A question asked with no answer expected.

setting The specific location or surroundings of a story.

subjective The feelings and ideas on the topic from the author's point of view.

submission A writing entry to be considered for publication.

synonym A word having the same, or nearly the same, meaning as another in the same language.

thesaurus A book of synonyms.

title The heading or name of a piece of writing.

tone A matter of expression showing a certain attitude or mood.

topic The subject of a piece of writing.

verb A word that shows action or links the subject to another word in the sentence.

For More Information

National Council of Teachers of English (NCTE)
Achievement Awards in Writing
1111 Kenyon Rd.
Urbana, IL 61801-1096
Web site: http://www.ncte.org

Reading, Writing, and Art Awards
Weekly Reader Corporation
200 First Stamford Pl.
P.O. Box 120023
Stamford, CT 06912-0023
Web site: http://
www.weeklyreader.com

Scholastic Art and Writing Awards
557 Broadway
New York, NY 10012
Web site:
http://www.www.scholastic.com

Web Sites

Due to the changing nature of Internet links, the Rosen Publishing Group, Inc., has developed an online list of Web sites related to the subject of this book. This site is updated regularly. Please use this link to access the list:

www.rosenlinks.com/lws/pewr

Index

About the Author

Lauren Spencer is originally from California and now lives in New York City, where she teaches writing workshops in the public schools. She also writes lifestyle and music articles for magazines.

Credits

Designer: Geri Fletcher; **Editor:** Joann Jovinelly